The Recipe for Real Happiness

Four Simple Ingredients

MELISSA GARSON
M.Ed., MAPP

First Edition: June 2018

Illustrations by Micaela Ezra
Interior design by Susannah Fears

For more information, visit melissagarson.com

Dedication

This book is dedicated to my mother, Joyce.

I have learned so much from her, some of which I want to emulate and some of which I don't. My mother wasn't perfect, but she did the best she could, and I was lucky to get the best of her.

I got her appreciation for natural beauty, her ability to entertain and make people feel comfortable. I'd also like to think that I got her simple, elegant style.

Many years ago, my mom told me that I should write a book. At the time I laughed and said, "Okay, Mom." I wasn't sure that would ever happen. But a week before she passed, I was able to tell her that my first book was going to be published, and that I was going to dedicate it to her.

Mom, I love you. This one's for you!

Contents

Introduction   **7**

Love   **13**

Gratitude   **41**

Mindfulness   **67**

Learning   **93**

Acknowledgments   **121**

Introduction

You and I are a lot alike. We have some good days and some not-so-good days. The difference between my days and yours is that I have learned not to linger in negative thoughts or emotions. Instead, I follow the advice I give to others so that I can fully appreciate all the natural beauty and different types of people that life has to offer. Essentially, I walk my own talk!

You are about to read the best and most effective life practices that I've carefully curated from many years of experience working with people and studying Positive Psychology at The University of Pennsylvania. Positive Psychology is the science of human flourishing. It is living a life filled with meaning and greater well-being—in essence, what makes people authentically happy.

Not everyone has the opportunity to listen and learn from the top researchers in this field, so it has become not only my passion but also my mission to share these tools. *The Recipe for Real Happiness*: *Four Simple Ingredients* will strengthen your "mental muscle" and put YOU in the driver's seat of your life.

If you want to hear people say, *"I'll have what she's having,"* or *"I want some of that positive energy,"* then keep reading.

People ask me all the time, "Were you always this happy and full of energy?" Honestly, the answer is a resounding no. When I was in my 20s, I remember feeling like I was on a hamster wheel, spinning faster and faster but going nowhere. I recall saying to a friend, as we were walking down a busy Manhattan street, "I want to feel my feet." I didn't even know what I meant, but I knew that I felt detached from my body, as if I were operating on automatic pilot. I was continually giving the power of my mental state over to the world around me. If things went well, I was happy. If they did not, I wasn't. I wanted to be more in control of my emotions, to live more consciously and more deliberately. I yearned to feel comfortable in my own skin and excited about my life.

Like you, I simply knew there was more to life than what I was experiencing, but I didn't have the mental capacity to gain control over my emotions. I finally got off the hamster wheel when I picked up *Learned Optimism* by Dr. Martin Seligman from the self-help section of my local bookstore. Little did I know that 20 years later, I would become his student. From his book, I learned that we have much more control over our level of optimism than we once thought. There was no stopping me after that. I sought out more books, videos, lectures—anything and everything I could find about becoming a more confident, more positive and happier person.

What started out as a quest for my personal emotional growth has now turned into my life's calling to share this knowledge with others. I have spent most of my adult life studying what makes people happy. I savor everyday experiences and live on a higher frequency: one of positivity. I gradually found my own way of living in happiness, and I promise, you can too.

I wrote *The Recipe for Real Happiness* to share the answers I've found. It is a culmination of scientifically proven techniques, expert insights, and simple everyday practices.

By nature, I am a teacher as well as an avid learner. My first career was teaching in a public school in the Bronx, New York. Years later, after I had my own two children, I attended a specialized Life Coaching program. I was so inspired by the work I was doing that I continued my education and received a second Master's degree in Applied Positive Psychology from the University of Pennsylvania.

As a Positive Psychology Life Coach for over a decade, I have helped hundreds of clients, many friends and family members, and even people I've met only briefly—taxi drivers, waiters, salespeople—discover ways of finding more meaning and contentment in their lives.

Now, don't get me wrong. The recipe in this book is not some magical immunization against tragedy and disaster. The same crappy stuff that happens to you also happens to me. I was in a bad car accident. My house caught on fire, I lost two dogs in one year, and so much more.

It's inevitable. Things won't always go the way you want them to. You are going to get upset; you are human. Real happiness is not about floating through life with smiley faces and rainbows. It's about bouncing back from disappointment and adversity so that you can fully appreciate and enjoy your life. You can achieve this by developing simple skills that are sustainable over time. Negative emotions are a natural part of our everyday lives. This book does not encourage you to attempt to eliminate negative feelings; instead, it enables you to counterbalance them with positivity.

So how do you combat feeling like you're always on the edge of something negative? This book will help you fill your emotional bank account with more positivity. That way, when you have a negative experience, you can make an easy withdrawal without feeling depleted. Being positive takes practice. *The Recipe for Real Happiness* will lay the groundwork of positivity so that you don't allow as much negativity to take up the precious real estate in your mind.

By following these practices, anyone can become happier, including you. You have more control over your emotions and well-being than you probably realize. It's entirely possible to retrain your brain to create new neural pathways and learn habits that will help you take charge of your own happiness.

Reading this book and applying these practices will put you on that path. *The Recipe for Real Happiness* is made up of **four essential ingredients**:

• **Love**: Cultivating and developing a deeper love for yourself, nurturing your relationships and opening your heart to new ways of expressing and receiving love.

• **Gratitude**: Appreciating yourself, the world around you and the people who make your life richer. Gratitude for the simple things generates a feeling of abundance.

• **Mindfulness**: Letting go of the past, not worrying about the future, and connecting with the present moment without judgment. Living mindfully is about being more conscious and developing greater awareness.

• **Learning**: Letting your experiences, good and bad, be your teacher and using what you've learned to help strengthen your emotional resilience. Opening yourself up to new opportunities, possibilities and different perspectives. This is also known as having a growth mindset.

Each ingredient is supported by ten practices that will help you stock up on emotional reserves. This will allow you to become the best, most fulfilled version of yourself. That way, when you face a setback, you'll be able to address it from a place of inner strength.

Each practice ends with a specific technique that you can easily incorporate into your daily life. All of the techniques build on each other, creating a solid foundation from which to live by.

The ingredients all blend together to help you become a better version of yourself. At different times of your life, you might need more of one ingredient than another—but having access to all four helps you call upon them whenever you need to.

This "cookbook" is more flexible than most others you may encounter because there's no proper order to use the ingredients. You may want to read the entire book through and then go back and begin doing the practices that best suit you. Maybe you're feeling adventurous and want to flip to a random page and pick up a technique to practice that day. Perhaps you would like to read the book with a group of friends and experiment different practices together. Take comfort in knowing that there will always be something here for you.

I encourage you to try all of the practices and choose the

ones that work best for you. You'll get the most from this book by truly making it your own. Grab your favorite pen or highlighter and get ready to underline, highlight, write comments and take notes. This does not have to be a one-time read. Keep it as a reference because we all need reminders from time to time.

The Recipe for Real Happiness is written with tremendous love for you, the reader. I sincerely hope it will help you become more positive and resilient. As your happiness guide and mentor, I encourage you to incorporate these practices into your daily life. Turn them into habits. You'll be happier, genuinely happier, before you know it!

Look in the mirror now. After you have embraced *The Recipe for Real Happiness*, you will look and feel differently about yourself and your life. Let's begin!

First Ingredient:

Love

Love

Love is one of the most profound emotions known to human beings. Living in love means making an ongoing, conscious effort to acknowledge the good in yourself and others. This naturally leads to feeling more positive about who you are and the world around you.

When I was younger, I wondered why being nice to people felt so natural and easy. What was my motivation? Was I trying to make people like me? I didn't quite understand why being generous and thoughtful felt so good. The reason finally became clear when I was studying for my master's degree. I discovered that one of my top character strengths is the capacity to love and be loved—after taking the fascinating "Values in Action Character Strengths Survey." I encourage you to take this survey too (you can find it on my website at https://www.melissagarson.com/learning) to learn what your strengths are! Studies have shown that using your strengths as much as possible, in new and different ways, is a pathway to feeling more fulfilled and engaged in life. It didn't matter whether I was being nice because I wanted to be liked or because it felt natural. My strength validated my desire to be nice and to live in love.

By learning to love, you can do good for others and reap the feel-good benefits just by doing it. The feeling and emotions associated with loving yourself and others will come with practice. Act as if you want to be more loving to your family and friends, more concerned about your neighbors, more considerate of your co-workers and kinder to strangers. Act as if you care; the more you practice it, the more you will.

Commit to living in love and then practice, practice, practice. In your own way, practice strengthening your capacity to see goodness in others. Practice ways you can help or make a difference in someone's life. Practice and acknowledge kindness that others extend to you. You will be rewarded with the feeling of living in love.

Each day, I live in love through lots of little moments. Whether I'm on the subway, at the dry cleaner, in a grocery store, working with a client or enjoying the company of friends and family, I seize every opportunity to be warm, kind and loving.

Living in love means accepting other people for who they are, with compassion. I've learned that when I quiet down my quick judgments of others, I am able see the common bonds of humanity. This makes it easier to love. By letting go of your judgments, you'll find that you are more similar to those around you. If people were more aware of these similarities, we'd all experience a greater capacity to love.

Living in love is also about accepting and believing in your own worthiness and knowing that others can recognize it too. I surround myself with supportive, caring people who accept me—imperfections and all. This has helped me to develop and honor who I really am.

Loving yourself is the foundation for loving others. That is why, as you'll find, these practices begin with and build on self-love. As you grow while living in love, you'll find a profound sense of both self-worth and connection with others. Even if you don't feel particularly lovable or loving, act as if you were, practice by practice, technique by technique. You'll soon be amazed at how good you will feel.

Let's start practicing!

10 Practices
to Love

Love Yourself

The most important relationship you will ever invest in is the one you have with yourself. Learning to accept, nurture and love yourself is essential to your happiness and well-being. Recognizing your own unique strengths and gifts can help you feel more confident and enable you to share your gifts with others.

You have within you special gifts and talents that are your very own. You were meant to share them. When you embrace your gifts and talents, and share them with others, you will feel a greater sense of empowerment and self-worth.

Help yourself uncover them. Why not? You will be living with yourself for the rest of your life!

Technique

Think of a time when you felt like you were you, at your best. What were you doing? Whom were you with? How were you feeling? What skills and strengths were you using?

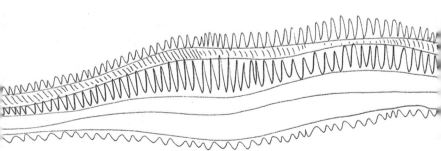

Write about it in detail. Label it the "Me at my best" sheet. This is something you can refer to when you need a little positive reminder of your self worth!

The next time you're tempted to criticize or belittle yourself, take out your "Me at my best" sheet and recall the best in yourself.

"Most of the shadows of this life are caused by standing in one's own sunshine."

- Ralph Waldo Emerson

Value What You Do

It is important to add meaning to anything that you do. Whether volunteering, caring for a family, being a student, or whatever your role is day-to-day, it is essential to do your best and take pride in it, always.

Recognize the value in the work that you put forth every day. It's important to acknowledge that regardless of whether it's big or small, you can have an impact on people.

Think about how what you do contributes to others. Rather than just seeing your job as a job, look at how it's actually making a difference for others. By actively noticing how your efforts are contributing to the greater good, you are valuing what you do. We find meaning in our jobs not by monetary compensation, but by measuring our value.

Oftentimes, it's difficult to feel inspired by your job. But once you look at how your work impacts others, you can start to fully appreciate and understand why your job matters.

Technique

Write a personal testimonial for yourself as a reminder of what you contribute to the world. Every task has a purpose, and there is none too menial to acknowledge. Remind yourself that your role is an important part of the bigger picture.

"Act as if what you do
makes a difference. It does."

- William James

Reach Out and Touch

A very powerful predictor of human happiness is the quality of our relationships. Cherish and nurture your connections. Make time for family and friends and new people that you meet along the way.

Staying in touch takes time and effort, but it's worth it! Don't worry about how many months or years it's been since you last talked. It's never too late to recharge or rekindle a relationship. When you invite people into your day for the sole purpose of keeping connected, this is truly living in love.

Technique

Pick up the phone and call a friend, relative or someone you care about. Drop a note or write an email to simply say, "Thinking of you."

The most impactful way to touch someone is with your personal presence—so make an effort to connect in person when you can.

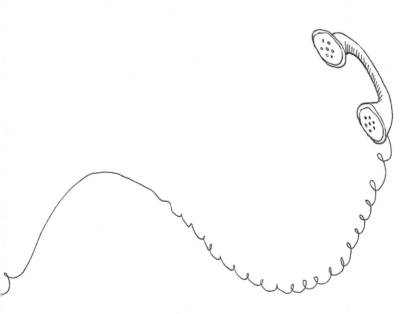

"If I had to summarize all the scientific literature
on the causes of human happiness in one word, that word
would be 'social.' We are by far the most social species
on Earth. Even ants have nothing on us. If I wanted to pre-
dict your happiness, I wouldn't want to know your gender,
religion, health, or income. I'd want to know about your
social network—about your friends and family
and the strength of your bonds with them."

- Daniel Gilbert

Talk Isn't Cheap

We live in a world where many people walk around looking down at their phone oblivious to those around them. Remember when people actually took time to talk and listen to one another? You never know what will come from a conversation. You may learn something about your family, make a friend, find an employer or even spark a romantic connection!

Talk to the people around you, wherever you are. You may be pleasantly surprised to see where the conversation takes you.

Technique

Seize everyday opportunities to connect with people. When you're standing in the supermarket checkout line, strike up a conversation with the person behind or in front of you. Look for a way to offer a sincere compliment. Make it a goal to talk to one stranger every day.

*"People may not remember exactly what you did,
or what you said, but they will always
remember how you made them feel."*

- Maya Angelou

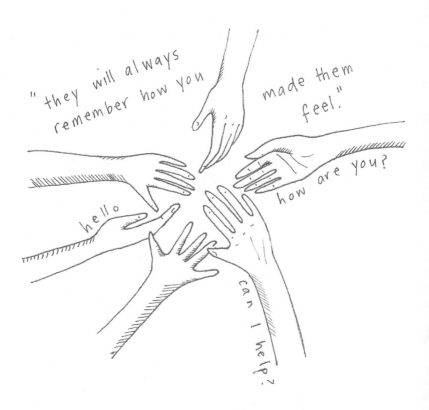

Hug Someone Today

Hugging is a powerful tool that not only changes the way you feel but also does the same for the person who is fortunate enough to get a hug from you. As they say, a hug goes both ways!

Oxytocin is the hormone secreted by the pituitary gland when we hug or touch someone, and it is often referred to as the "love hormone." It can reduce your level of stress and even lower your blood pressure. Give more hugs and focus on how good they can make you feel both physically and emotionally.

Technique

Make time to hug your loved ones good morning and good night. Ask for a hug goodbye before you leave the house and a hug hello when you come home. When someone looks like needs a hug, have the courage to ask, "Could I give you a hug?"

"A hug, pat on the back, and even a friendly hand-shake are processed by the reward center in the central nervous system, which is why they can have a powerful impact on the human psyche, making us feel happiness and joy. And it doesn't matter if you're the toucher or touchee. The more you connect with others—on even the smallest physical level—the happier you'll be."

- Shekar Raman

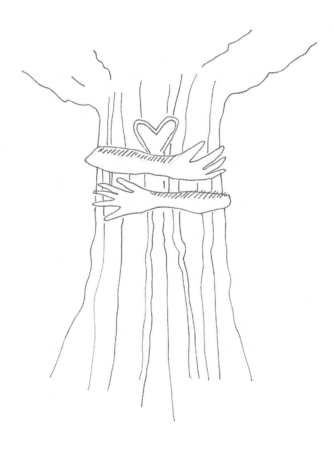

Get High on Helping

Be kind! When you are kind and compassionate to another person, your brain's pleasure and reward centers react the same way as if you were the recipient of the good deed. Psychologists call this release of dopamine the "helper's high."

You don't have to be wealthy to give generously. Even small gestures like saying something thoughtful, holding open a door, offering to carry someone's heavy package or smiling at a stranger can make you feel good. "Aim high" by being kind and spreading joy to others. Every interaction with someone can be an opportunity to positively impact both of your lives.

Technique

Be on the lookout for ways to be kind. Do at least one small act of kindness every day. Encourage others to do the same.

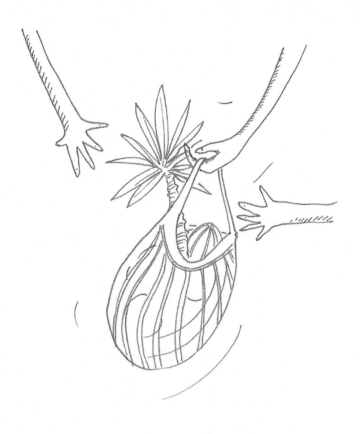

"If someone were to pay you ten cents
for every kind word you said about people and
collect five cents for every unkind word,
would you be rich or poor?"

- Anonymous

Choose Your Friends Wisely

Surround yourself with people who have your back, listen to you, believe in you and make you feel good about who you are.

Nourish your friendships. Experiencing genuine friendships can help ward off depression, boost your self-esteem and provide support in good and bad times.

Spend as little time as possible with people who are emotional vampires–the people who zap your energy and leave you feeling depleted and down.

Building genuine friendships can take time and hard work, but once those people are in your life, you will have built an entire support system. A good way to initially find those people is to recognize if they share common values with you. The more time you spend with uplifting people, the more joy you'll have in your life.

Technique

Get out your calendar and make plans to spend time with people who enrich, enlighten and energize you.

"Some cause happiness wherever they go;
others whenever they go."

- Oscar Wilde

Live With Purpose

Many people struggle to find that one thing that they are meant to do. Their "life purpose" may seem unattainable or elusive. Trying to find that reason to get up in the morning can sometimes be overwhelming. You may feel stuck if it doesn't come to mind easily; we all do at times.

People who are in touch with their passions–even the little ones—and who, as a result, are doing things that they love, are living their lives with purpose. Happiness is more than momentary pleasure; it's many moments linked together by purposeful actions. Don't forget, even the small actions count too!

Technique

Embrace the idea that fulfilling your passion(s) in life IS your purpose.

What inspires you? Is there some activity that motivates you and that you want to experience more in your life? Turn your hobby into your greatest passion. Writing? Teaching? Cooking? Gardening? Whatever it is, just do one thing today and you have already started.

> *"The ancient Greek definition of happiness*
> *was the full use of your powers along*
> *the lines of excellence."*

- John F. Kennedy

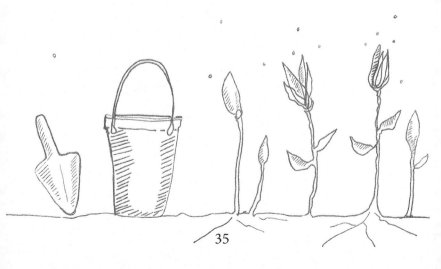

Smile

When you smile, you appear more approachable and friendly. You can almost feel it when someone is smiling when talking on the phone. Smiling can help shift your brain into a more positive mindset.

A smile triggers the release of the body's natural feel-good chemicals, benefitting both your mental and physical well-being. When people see you smile, they naturally have the urge to smile back. It's contagious, but in a good way! Smiling helps create stronger bonds in your relationships.

Technique

There is no single, simple gesture you can make that has as high-yield results as smiling. Open up, let your guard down, and smile at three people today. See what happens and notice how you feel.

"Sometimes your joy is the source of your smile, but sometimes your smile can be the source of your joy."

- Thich Nhat Hanh

Let Go of the Grudge

Forgiving is a gift you give to yourself. Forgiveness of people for the pain they have inflicted or harm they have caused you can free you from anger, hurt, disappointment and a lifetime of misery. It makes room for more love and inner peace in your life.

Whether it's a little spat or a long-held resentment toward someone, unresolved conflict can affect your mood and your health. Through forgiveness, you can find peace even though you've been wronged. You may be feeling angry and that's normal, but don't linger there.

Forgiveness is solely for your benefit. No one else even has to know about your decision to forgive.

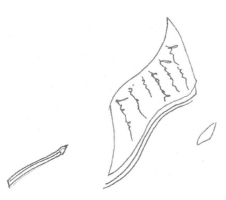

Technique

Confronting the issue can be very healing. If you're not ready, you can still find a way to release the burden. Write a letter to the person, stating your anger, hurt, resentment and frustration. You don't need to mail it. You'll be amazed at how putting pen to paper can help you let go and feel the benefits of forgiveness.

> *"Forgiveness is not always easy. At times, it feels*
> *more painful than the wound we suffered,*
> *to forgive the one that inflicted it. And yet,*
> *there is no peace without forgiveness."*
>
> - Marianne Williamson

Second Ingredient:

Gratitude

Gratitude

Living in gratitude means intentionally appreciating the various people and experiences in your life, both positive AND negative. By actively practicing gratitude, you see the value of everything in your life. As a result, you will enjoy life more. You will also create a protective emotional shield against toxic people and difficult situations. Think of it as an insurance policy that strengthens your mental immunity for those times when inevitable obstacles arise.

Practicing a deep sense of gratitude has been proven to be a very reliable method for increasing life satisfaction. Challenging situations lose their power to drag you down a spiral of disappointment or depression. People who regularly practice gratitude are healthier, happier, kinder and more compassionate. They tend to take better care of themselves, have better relationships and higher levels of self-esteem. Naturally, when you look for the good in everything and everyone, life becomes a lot sweeter!

You may feel grateful and consider yourself to be a grateful person, but do you consciously seek out things to be grateful for? For example, consider grocery shopping. When was the last time you went grocery shopping and thought, "How lucky am I to have this incredible selection of food right at my fingertips, and have the money to pay for it?"

For me, living in gratitude has become my default setting. When I show my gratitude for others, they feel appreciated and shower gratitude right back at me. It creates a continuous circle of gratitude. Becoming mindful and appreciative of moments—both big and small—that you are grateful for will help you build the strength and resilience you need to face life's challenges. The following practices will help you become an active seeker, a hunter and gatherer of things to be grateful for.

Let's start practicing!

10 Practices
to Gratitude

Grab Your Gratitude Glasses

Grateful people are happier people. Happiness isn't necessarily having what you want—it is appreciating what you have. Why not look for every opportunity to be grateful?

You can always find something to be grateful for—a good meal, a loving friend. Or simply pause to appreciate being alive. If you look at your life through a lens of gratitude rather than focusing on what may be missing, you will feel happier and more fulfilled.

Technique

Close your eyes. Imagine yourself wearing gratitude glasses. Open your eyes and look around...Your new "glasses" may transform the things you would normally take for granted and enable you to see them through more appreciative eyes.

*"It is impossible to feel grateful
and depressed in the same moment."*

- Naomi Williams

"Some people grumble that roses have thorns;
I am grateful that thorns have roses."

- Alphonse Karr

Gravitate Toward Grateful People

Grateful people are people who see the glass half full and look for the silver lining in everything. They are more fun to be around, and they make you feel better by being in their company.

People who are grateful know how to make the best out of any situation—whether it's positive or negative. Notice how you feel when you are with someone who is appreciative.

Technique

Seek out and surround yourself with those exuding the energy of gratefulness. We all know someone who effortlessly displays gratitude through little actions like thanking a stranger who opened the door or writing quick appreciation texts to friends and family members. If you know people like that, reach out to them. Make a plan to get together. Watch and learn from the way they perceive and interact with the world. If you don't know a grateful person, then become a gratitude spotter and look for strangers behaving gratefully. That's how you generate gratitude!

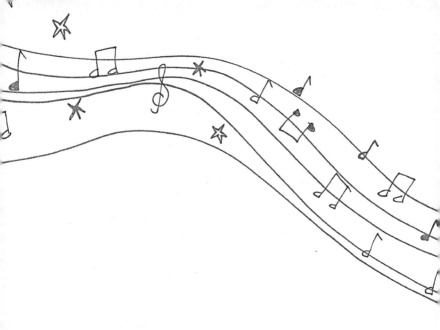

Let Music into Your Life

Music enhances life. It can elevate your mood, help alleviate stress and lessen depression. Music can motivate you to exercise, do housework or just dance around.

Music is used around the world as a powerful, natural spirit-lifter and a way to express feelings and connect with others. Don't let a day go by without enjoying music.

Technique

Create your own playlists of songs. If you look online, you can find hundreds of playlists for all your different moods. If you're feeling nostalgic, listen to music from your past that makes you smile.

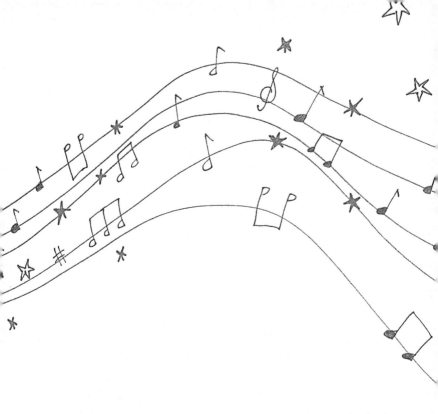

"*Music gives a soul to the universe,
wings to the mind, flight to the imagination
and life to everything.*"

- Plato

Savor It Out Loud

If you experience something you enjoy or appreciate, savor it and say it out loud. Whether you're with close friends, in a crowd of strangers or even if you're alone, go ahead and express your appreciation. It's a simple form of gratitude everyone can practice.

Happiness is a lot more than having positive experiences. It's also about noticing, enjoying and prolonging those experiences.

Verbalizing what you are feeling out loud allows you to linger in the experience longer. If others hear you, they might be inspired and enjoy your experience as well.

Technique

The next time you catch yourself thinking, "Wow" about something, don't hold back. Just say it out loud.

"Feeling gratitude and not expressing it is like wrapping a present and not giving it."

- William Arthur Ward

Less Is More

Abundance is a state of mind. We often think that if a little is good, then more is better. We wind up surrounded by excess "stuff" that we no longer use and enjoy.

Whether it's your desk, your kitchen, a closet or your car, a filled-up, busy environment can interfere with your inner peace.

Getting rid of the clutter will literally lighten up your life and help you appreciate what you have chosen to keep. Gratitude for what you already have and the power to appreciate it, fosters a feeling of satisfaction and contentment.

Technique

Get out your calendar and set aside one hour to start decluttering. Ask yourself, "Have I used this in the past year?" If not, it's time to pass it along. Choose to keep the item, sell it or give it away. If you are not keeping it, let someone else have the opportunity to enjoy the things you no longer need.

"The home is the center of your soul;
it's a total reflection of your inner life."

- Alexandra Stoddard

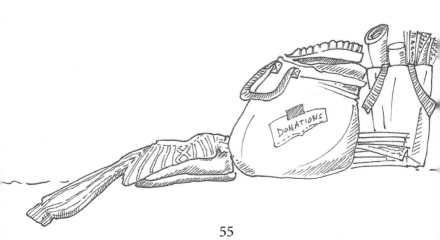

Write a Gratitude Letter

Expressing gratitude in writing is very powerful. This is different from a "Thank You" note. It is a sincere, heartfelt expression. Taking time to put your thoughts on paper allows you to elaborate on how someone's kindness, action or presence has made an impact upon your life. In an age when we're constantly texting and not paying attention to the world around us, a letter is often an unexpected surprise and a generous way to show appreciation.

This will not only be a mood-lifter for you, but also an emotional boost for the receiver.

Technique

Write a letter of gratitude to someone who has made a difference in your life and let him or her know what you are grateful for. It can be a relative, friend, teacher or even your child. Describe the effect that he or she had on you. Be as specific as you can. Notice how you feel while writing it.

"The deepest craving of human nature is
the need to be appreciated."

- William James

*"If the only prayer you say in your life is
'thank you' that would suffice."*

- Meister Eckhart

Accept, Appreciate, and Give Compliments

A compliment is a verbal gift. When you deny a compliment, it is an insult to the giver. When you accept a compliment, it's an acknowledgment. When you give a compliment, it is a gift to both of you.

It's not so easy to accept compliments. It may seem vain and conceited; yet, receiving them is a sign of confidence and grace.

When we pay a compliment to someone, we feel good about ourselves by making another person feel better.

Technique

When you receive a compliment of any kind, just say, "thank you." Start looking for genuinely nice things to say to people. It will become automatic and authentic. Give three compliments today. Watch peoples' faces light up when you compliment them. A few nice words can really be a tremendous boost!

wise lovely witty funny delightful insig thoughtful Extraordinar exciting amazing Bold grac

Express Your Gratitude

Whenever you feel grateful for something somone has said or done, make sure you share your gratitude. Stop, take a minute and show your appreciation.

When you share positivity with others, both you and the person you are appreciating share what is known as a "micro-moment" of love. You are creating a momentary emotional connection. This is a practice that you can cultivate. These moments can make you not only happier but healthier as well.

Technique

Pay attention and look for the things that others do for you. Share your gratitude. Sincerely tell others how much you appreciate them. Say an extra big "thank you" every time someone says or does something nice for you today. You'll feel good and they will too.

interesting resilient strong radian
brave kind generous awesome spirited
supportive unique courageou
mbitious loving authentic
heartfelt creativ
ingenious

"No one who achieves success does so
without acknowledging the help of others.
The wise and confident acknowledge
this help with gratitude."

- Alfred North Whitehead

Grow Gratitude through Journaling

Keeping a gratitude journal will help you focus on the good in your life. If you look for the good, you will find it. Journaling makes it easier to identify gratitude when you are actively seeking it on a daily basis. Gratitude tends to grow when you have a resource to refer back to when you most need the reminder!

When you seek out moments for which to be grateful, no matter how big or small, things in life become more meaningful. It's a shift in your attitude. It helps you linger on the positive and enjoy an experience again and again.

Technique

Get yourself a notebook and start writing. At the end of each day, write three things you are grateful for.

"As long as you are breathing, there is more right with you than there is wrong."

- Jon Kabat-Zinn

Enjoy the Natural World

Mother Nature is brilliant when it comes to soothing frazzled nerves and banishing the blues. Embrace the feeling you get when you observe the clouds above, the trees blowing in the breeze, the flowers blooming and the butterflies fluttering. Sunshine and natural light provide us with vitamin D, which is known to uplift and enhance our mood. That's nature's gift to you!

Doctors actually write "nature prescriptions" for people because it can be so healing. We spend our days in front of computer screens, on our phones or binge-watching TV shows which can lead to anxiety and depression. We often forget how amazing the universe is.

Technique

Go outside for a five-minute nature break. Do this with no real agenda. Take a walk and look up at the sky. When you

are inside, take nature breaks by looking out a window that overlooks plants and trees. Appreciate the natural beauty that is available to you at all times.

"If you truly love nature, you will find beauty everywhere."

- Vincent van Gogh

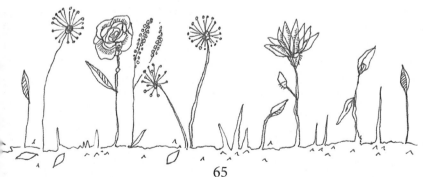

Third Ingredient:

Mindfulness

Mindfulness

For 20 years, I had "learn to meditate" as one of my New Year's resolutions. I used to find myself mentally and physically exhausted going from place to place and from one activity to the next. I had constant chatter reverberating in my mind, and it wasn't productive. I wanted to stop "winging" my life.

I wasn't quite sure why, but meditation seemed like the answer I was looking for: a calmer, more confident, centered feeling. I owned many books on learning how to meditate which were hidden under my skirt—the one on my night table. And there they sat, year after year. I was yearning for a way to be more present, to worry less, and simply enjoy my life more. Collecting meditation books did not bring me the peace I was looking for.

I didn't know it at the time, but what I wanted most was to become mindful. Mindfulness is living in the "now" moment and not dwelling in the past or worrying about the future. Practicing mindfulness is one of the most effective ways to increase your happiness.

Living mindfully is a philosophy. There are formal and informal mindfulness practices. We typically think of meditation as a formal practice, but informally practicing mindfulness will bring astounding benefits to your everyday life.

By becoming aware of the things that are happening in the present moment, without the lens of judgment, you are being mindful. Mindfulness is living each day with an open mind and an open heart, unencumbered by negative, emotional baggage or fear of what may or may not happen. The insights gained from living in the present moment will help you increase awareness of what causes you stress and anxiety, and, therefore, help you to return to balance more quickly.

In an effort to slow down and deepen my practice, I've gone on several silent retreats. Yes, silent: No talking for seven days. For a girl who cannot stay quiet in the dentist's chair, this was a challenge which made no sense to my friends and family. They were right to be skeptical, but I was determined. With the help of instruction, I quieted my anxieties and before long, I got comfortable with observing, reflecting and just being—all without the need to talk. These retreats inherently put a magnifying glass on my everyday thoughts and judgments. They also increased the intensity of my five senses as I became more aware of the sounds, smells, tastes, sights and textures that surrounded me.

Although the quiet experience worked for me, you don't have to go on a long, silent retreat or move to a monastery with Buddhist monks to bring balance and inner peace to your life. Mindfulness isn't something you need to fit into your busy schedule or someplace you need to get to. I love the saying, "Bliss is a constant state of mind, undisturbed by gain or loss." It is simply a way of being, of cultivating acceptance for the way things are.

Think about how everything feels when you first fall in love. Food tastes better, the words to music become more meaningful, and colors appear brighter. The world becomes a welcoming place. That's what becoming mindful—living in the moment—does for you. To live mindfully is to fall in love with life. It's amazing and it's simple. But it does take practice.

Let's start practicing!

10 Practices
to Mindfulness

Press the Pause Button

Things don't always go the way we want them to. When you feel frenzied, challenged or uncomfortable, imagine pushing a mental pause button. Even in the midst of chaos or stress, you can reach for your pause button to help bring you into the present moment and become more mindful.

Learning to pause gives you the opportunity to take a step back to choose how you want to respond rather than just reacting to a situation. Pausing helps you calm down, get centered, gather yourself and operate from a more conscious state of mind.

Technique

Create a visual image of your pause button. Picture what it looks like in your mind. Remember that it's there and at your fingertips!

> *"Between stimulus and response there is a space.*
> *In that space is our power to choose our response.*
> *In our response lies our growth and our freedom."*
>
> - Viktor Frankl

Acknowledge, Accept, Act

Taking steps toward making positive change isn't always easy. You may find yourself stuck and conflicted about how to move forward. Here's a mindfulness practice that will make it easier for you to get unstuck:

Give your issues the respect they deserve. By acknowledging them, you take away the power they hold over you. When you accept and stop resisting your problems, you can then actually deal with them. Once you've acknowledged and accepted your situation, you can then take action.

Technique

Use the 3 'A's: **Acknowledge, Accept** and **Act**.
Acknowledge a situation that you are in today. **Accept** that this is the way it is now. Once you have really accepted it and tried not to push it away, choose one action that you can take that will move you closer toward your desired outcome. **Act** on it!

"*Stop resisting your problems so furiously in your mind. Stop struggling to solve them. If you do that, a great sense of peace followed by a great sense of power will come to you.*"

- Norman Vincent Peale

Leave Your Baggage Behind

Carrying around emotional baggage can cause anxiety, embarrassment, guilt, anger and a plethora of other negative feelings. This emotional baggage is often called your "story." Maybe yours is a carry-on bag; maybe it's a suitcase; maybe it's a steamer trunk. It's okay. We all have a past—but you don't have to carry it around with you everywhere you go.

Your past does not have to dictate your future. In fact, the practice of mindfulness leaves no room for overhead luggage!

Technique

Put a rubber band on your wrist. Whenever your inner voice brings back your old story, snap the band to remind you to drop the suitcase—it isn't serving you! Imagine walking away from the baggage carousel free from all that extra weight, heading toward the future you want to create.

"In the process of letting go you will
lose many things from the past,
but you will find yourself."

- Deepak Chopra

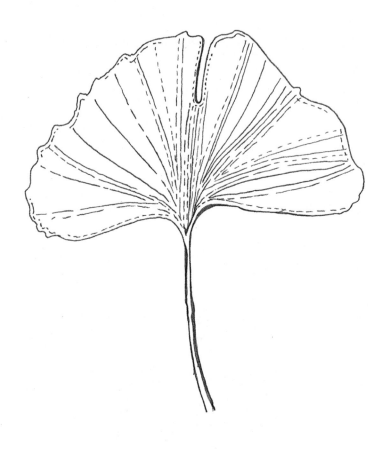

"Freedom is the only worthy goal in life.
It is won by disregarding things that
lie beyond our control."

- Epictetus

Embrace the Serenity Prayer

The Serenity Prayer is a prayer that can help you find your inner peace:

*Grant me the serenity to accept
the things I cannot change,*

*the courage to change the things I can,
and the wisdom to know the difference.*

- Reinhold Niebuhr

The words in this prayer are not only about acceptance but also empowerment. It reminds us that there are many things in life we cannot control or change. It encourages us to take action when we can.

Technique

Learn these words and call upon them during stressful situations. You can write them down and keep them as a reminder whenever you find yourself overwhelmed. This will help you find serenity in that moment and strengthen your capacity to achieve a greater sense of inner peace. When something is bothering you, ask yourself, "What part of this do I actually have control over?" Do what you can, and let go of what you can't. Find your serenity in the present moment.

Be In Your "Now"

As you go about your day, get out of your head and be in your now. This can inspire you to respect every moment that you're blessed with.

If you are making a meal, embrace the smells and the textures of the ingredients. In the shower, relax and enjoy the warm water on your skin. When you are commuting to and from work, look out the window and see the world as you move through it.

Technique

Pick one thing that you will do today and focus your complete attention on it. Embrace your five senses to bring you fully into your body, so that you can become grounded in the present moment.

"Mindfulness is simply being aware of what is happening right now without wishing it were different; enjoying the pleasant without holding on when it changes (which it will); being with the unpleasant without fearing it will always be this way (which it won't)."

- James Baraz

Mindfully Breathe (4-7-8)

Living mindfully is meditation in action. There are a variety of mindful meditations. This one (from Dr. Andrew Weil) is a specific mindfulness practice that involves consciously focusing on your breath and calming down your nervous system. When your mind is frantic, your breathing becomes shallow. When you concentrate on your breath, your mind can become quieter. When your mind settles, you are able to get some space around your thoughts and be less anxious which allows you to think more clearly.

This practice slows down your breathing, relieves stress and can help improve your sleep.

Make mindful breathing a daily ritual—even if you have only a few minutes. You will feel a sense of accomplishment and control over your well-being in a way that you never thought possible!

Technique

Set a timer for three minutes and sit comfortably with your spine as straight as possible. This will allow you to breathe more fully. Place your hand on your belly, and as you breathe in, make sure your belly (not your chest) rises. Remove your hand and place both hands comfortably in your lap. After a few breaths, take a deep breath in for four counts, hold for seven counts, and breathe out for eight counts.

Do this every day for at least three minutes.

*"Feelings come and go like clouds in a windy sky.
Conscious breathing is my anchor."*

- Thich Nhat Hanh

Take a Tech Break

Break free from technology before it breaks you. The constant need to check email or social media can become addicting and cause tremendous emotional stress. Using electronics has been linked to hand, joint, tendon problems, eye strain, difficulty focusing, and pain in your neck area.

Technology can take you away from being in the present moment and connecting with other human beings. Instead of engaging with strangers while we're waiting in line, we automatically pick up our phones to read texts or check Instagram and Facebook. We miss so much as a result!

As you go through your day, take the opportunity to disconnect from technology and reconnect with the real world. Put your phone away.

Technique

Take tech breaks throughout your day. Choose a specific, regularly scheduled time and turn off all your devices. Move away from the computer; put your phone down. Take a walk; look around you. Enjoy a breath of fresh air. For the ultimate tech break, when you go to bed, power off all your devices and put them in another room.

"The difference between technology and slavery is that slaves are fully aware that they are not free."

- Nassim Nicholas Taleb

"The ability to simplify means to eliminate the
unnecessary so that the necessary may speak."

- Hans Hofmann

Leave Space in Your Schedule

Give yourself room to breathe during your day. Instead of rushing from one activity to another, allow yourself some time to fully savor each activity that you're doing. We so often feel like we are running against the clock. Work, errands, chores, caring for others... our days turn out to be one long laundry list of activities.

One of the keys to being mindful is to enjoy each experience fully. It doesn't matter if you're doing the dishes or if you're stuck in traffic, there are little things that you can do to actively appreciate your life. Not only does leaving space in your schedule give you more time to experience life, it also gives you the opportunity to connect with others, be more creative and operate from a more relaxed place.

When making plans or scheduling events, don't overbook yourself. Leave space in your schedule and give yourself the gift of mindful moments!

Technique

Make changes in your calendar to be sure that you have dedicated enough time for each event. If events do overlap, try to reschedule or prioritize them to minimize your stress. Schedule in "free time" on a weekly basis. Add an extra five minutes for everything you plan to do. This extra space in your schedule will give you time to complete your tasks without rushing to start the next thing.

Eat More Consciously

Eating is a great way to practice being mindful. We all have to eat, and we tend to take the experience for granted. We often couple eating with another activity. We eat when we are reading, watching television, typing on the computer or gazing at our smartphones. As a result, we don't even taste our food, let alone enjoy the flavors of it.

When you eat or drink, try to slow down the process. Give the entire experience your full attention. Use your senses. Notice the smell, texture, color and the flavors of what you are eating.

You may find that you will not only enjoy your food more, but you may also eat less and make healthier choices too!

Technique

Begin by devoting one meal to eating mindfully. As you eat, ask yourself: Am I tasting what I'm eating? Pause in between bites; put your fork down. Focus on the flavor, the aroma and the texture of what you are eating. Notice how this meal makes you feel.

"When walking, walk.
When eating, eat."

- Zen Proverb

Fourth Ingredient:

Learning

Learning

The first three ingredients combine to make you feel more centered and strong. This last foundation, which is also related to the "growth mindset," is like the fourth leg of a chair. It allows you to feel more balanced and able to withstand whatever comes up without toppling over!

Look at your life as though it were a classroom full of lessons and opportunities for growth. All of the lessons you need to learn will be presented to you. Naturally, some of them will be more difficult than others. Know that, with practice and effort, you can change your brain and feel more competent and resilient in the face of life's challenges. All of these lessons are extremely important for your own personal growth. Whatever you may be facing right now, in the present moment, there is a teaching moment waiting to happen.

Living in Learning Mode means seeing life's challenges—as well as its joys—as chances to learn. Whether learning from success, adventures, mistakes, loss, illness or everyday life experiences—keep learning. This mode can help you see life as more interesting, and its disappointments and failures as less devastating. Getting discouraged by setbacks is one of the most common reasons people say they give up.

When things don't go the way you intended, resist the urge to focus on what went wrong. Instead, learn to embrace setbacks as part of your overall journey and re-frame obstacles as learning opportunities. Research has shown that people who have this perspective are more likely to persevere than those who get overly frustrated by adversity. You can't control life's setbacks, but you can control your reactions to them. This gives you a sense of personal control. Feeling as though you are a student of the universe allows you to react to circumstances with determination, hope and resilience.

I have been living in Learning Mode for quite some time, and it has become automatic. I no longer beat myself up for choices that don't turn out the way I want them to. I seek out information on how to use situations to help me make different choices in the future.

I got into the habit of asking myself, "What can I learn from this experience?" and "What knowledge can I use going forward?" As research has shown—and as I know from years of personal and professional experience—having a learning mindset helps you feel more optimistic, improves your sense of self-worth and enriches your relationships. What's more, embracing continuous learning is restorative; it can help you come back into balance and enjoy your life more.

Living in Learning Mode is to live with a mind that is open to learning from all your experiences—the rewarding and the challenging, the joyful and the painful.

Let's start practicing!

10 Practices
to Learning

It's Not What You Know, It's How You Grow

You can choose to have a growth mindset. This view creates a love of learning and an inner strength that is essential to being your best self and having a happier approach to life. When you do this, you remove limits on what you think you can learn and achieve. You'll be able to open the door to endless possibilities.

Those with a growth mindset realize that their talents and abilities can be developed. With the right focus and repetition, our brains can create new neural pathways that result in new skills, knowledge and habits. No matter how young or old you are, keep your mind open to learning.

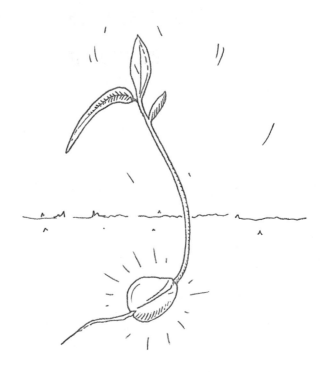

Technique

Today, catch yourself being your own inner critic and telling yourself that you'll never be able to do this or that. Would you tell someone you love, "You'll never be able to do that, you may as well give up"? So stop saying that to yourself.

Instead say, "I may not be able to do this yet, but I know that if I invest time and energy into it, I can learn it." Shift those restraining thoughts. Recognize that you have choices in how you see the world and your potential.

> *"I don't divide the world into the weak and*
> *the strong, or the successes and the failures...*
> *I divide the world into the learners*
> *and the non-learners."*

> – Benjamin Barber

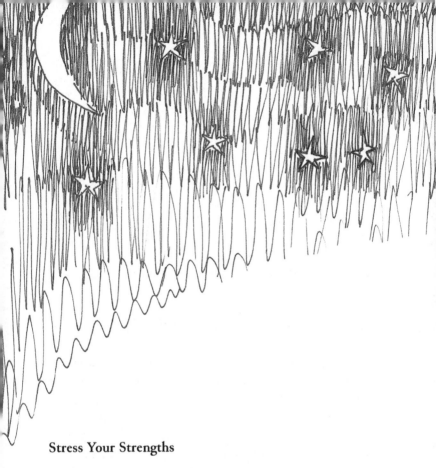

Stress Your Strengths

Using your strengths is key to finding success and happiness. You can identify a strength by the way you feel when practicing it. It feels natural. You may feel "in the zone" and lose track of time. Find your strength where the level of challenge and your ability meet the "sweet spot."

When you are working from your strengths, you become more inspired, energized and empowered. This is one of the best ways to build confidence and feel more secure.

Technique

Recall a setback from a time in your life when you dealt with a difficult situation and you used your strengths to get through it. Write down any of the strengths that you think may have helped you.

Use those same strengths to help you get through whatever challenges you may be facing now. Reflecting on past success is a great way to live in learning mode!

"Find your own 'sweet spot.' Take your talents and enjoy them, share them, expand them."

- Kofi Awoonor

It's Okay to Say, "I Don't Know"

When faced with a dilemma when you don't know what to do or how to answer a question, find the courage to say, "I don't know." These three words can bring you a sense of relief and profound peacefulness.

People who are perfectionists have a tendency to view "not knowing" as a weakness. It is actually a strength. One of the keys to living a happy life is to be able to differentiate between what you know and what you don't.

Not always having the answer allows you to be more open and to learn from those around you. It's okay to ask for help.

Technique

Practice letting go of the need to know. Think of a time when you were involved in a situation and you pretended to "know" something instead of being honest and allowing yourself to "not know." How did you feel? It is far more empowering to be honest and accept that we can't know everything. If you are in a situation in which you feel uncertain, or if someone asks you a question that you don't have the answer to, simply say, "I don't know."

I don't know

"Being entirely honest
with oneself is a good exercise."

- Sigmund Freud

Set Goals for Yourself

When you live in Learning Mode, you are consistently growing. As a learner, you develop the ability to dance with life and enjoy the journey.

When you set goals for yourself, it's all about identifying specific outcomes and how you intend to accomplish them. When goals are vague, they're easier to put off and harder to accomplish. You can't get what you want if you don't know what it is you want.

Technique

Write down one simple goal. Make sure it's specific, measurable, realistic and timely. For instance, if you don't want to be stuck in a job that makes you unhappy, identify how you could do to remedy the situation. List three baby steps to get you started. Share it with someone.

When you've accomplished your goal, congratulate yourself! Celebrate! And then set another goal.

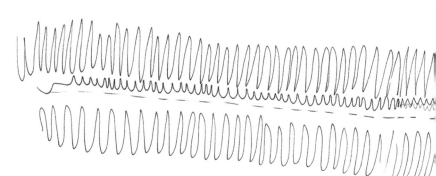

"A journey of a thousand miles begins with a single step."

- Lao Tzu

Purposeful Passion

You can find purpose in your passions. Your passion is something you get so involved with that you lose track of time. It makes your eyes light up and people tell you they notice how excited you are when you talk about it.

What are you good at? People who spend time doing what they love while sharing these experiences with others are living with purpose. Let go of the fear that stops you from being who you really are and take the first step toward living with purpose.

Technique

Make a list of what you loved doing as a child. What do you do now that truly engages you? This is your passion list. Look at your list every day, and find a way to do at least one thing that brings you joy.

*"He who has a why to live
can bear almost any how."*

- Friedrich Nietzsche

Embrace the Empowerment of Change

Strengthening your ability to accept change can be very liberating. Possessing the inner sense of competence and flexibility is incredibly empowering. Change is inevitable, but not always easy when we are attached to people, things and situations.

Most people do not invite change into their lives, but nonetheless, it occurs. Understanding that all things change will help you recognize the importance of enjoying and experiencing life as it is happening. Change is not your enemy. It just is.

Technique

Notice that change is occurring all of the time. To be alive is to be in constant change. Practice being flexible and accepting change instead of fighting against it. Remind yourself that everything is impermanent.

When you acknowledge your experience and honor the feelings you have, you are, in essence, accepting change—even though it may take time to really embrace it.

"The only thing that is constant is change."

- Heraclitus

Name Your Negatives

It is important to remember that we are human beings and we feel both positive and negative emotions. It's natural to feel angry, sad, upset and sorry at times. We need to allow ourselves to experience our negative emotions without allowing them to linger within us for too long. Ruminating on them can create a downward spiral of increasing negativity.

We cannot control what emotions we will experience next, but we can choose how we respond to them. Allow yourself to feel your emotions. Don't sweep them under the rug. This will give you a chance to understand and process your feelings in a healthy manner. Remember, you are just feeling these emotions; YOU are not the emotion itself.

Technique

Remember the last time you felt upset. Relive the experience, close your eyes and notice what you are feeling in your body, especially in your neck , shoulders, chest and stomach. Label what you're feeling: I feel angry; I feel confused; I feel betrayed.

Putting words to your feelings can give you some distance from the intensity of the emotion. The next time you are feeling angry, sad or anxious label your feelings. "I feel_____.
This allows you to feel more separate from the emotion and to respond intentionally, rather than reacting automatically and unconsciously.

> *"We cannot ignore our pain and feel compassion for it at the same time. Mindfulness requires that we not 'over-identify' with thoughts and feelings, so that we are caught up and swept away by negativity."*
>
> - Brené Brown

Life as Your Classroom

Everything you experience is ultimately an opportunity for learning. We all face difficult situations and challenging times; however, the way you perceive them can either help or hinder you.

This is true no matter what the circumstances are. When you adopt a learning mindset, there is something to be learned from everything. You attach meaning to experiences, gather information and come to see things in a new light.

Learning from your experiences helps you gain a wealth of knowledge from which you can draw from in your future. When you have a mindset of living in learning, it makes your life more meaningful.

Technique

Review a past experience and consider, "What did I learn?" "How will I use this going forward?" Then, as you go through your day, apply the lessons you learned from the past to your various new experiences.

"Everything is either an opportunity to grow,
or an obstacle to keep you from growing.
You get to choose."

- Wayne W. Dyer

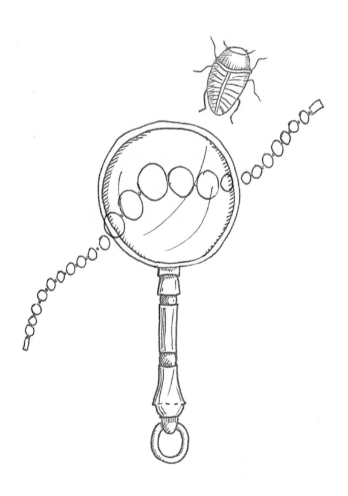

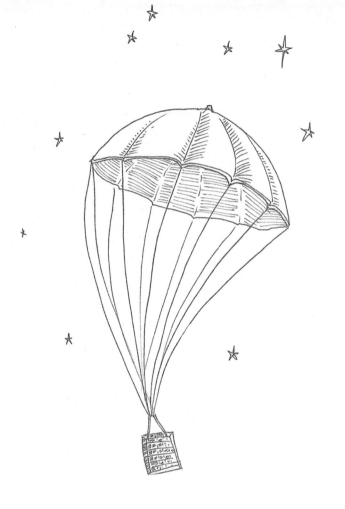

"The mind is like a parachute.
It works best when it is open."

- Unknown

Get Curious

As a child, curiosity was one of your greatest teachers! Curiosity is what allowed you to learn how to live in the world. Continue to cultivate your curiosity and keep learning. Become more curious and you'll become more interested—and more interesting.

Curious people are better listeners. They are more receptive to learning and exploration. When you're inquisitive, you can strengthen your relationships, increase your brain activity and feel good about yourself!

Technique

What is something you've always wanted to do or know more about? Nurture and develop your curiosity. Ask more questions. Sign up for a course in something new that interests you such as interior design, how to use your computer—or perhaps a meditation class. Always be willing to learn something new. Open up and get curious!

Be a Lifetime Student

Consider the people you interact with and the situations you find yourself in your teachers. You're a student in the school of life! Everyone and everything is there to teach you something and can be an instrument for growth.

If you find yourself getting annoyed with someone, or if a friend expresses an opinion that you disagree with, look at it as your chance to exercise some tolerance and possibly see things from a different perspective.

When you see life as your classroom, everything becomes more animated with possibility and potential. It may be a lesson for you.

Technique

Take yourself mentally back to the last time you felt impatient or irritated. Visualize the person or situation in front of you as your teacher. What are they trying to teach you? What do you need to learn? As you go through life, you can choose to learn from negative feelings or emotions, instead of being controlled by them.

Humanity is my teacher

"All the world is my school and all
humanity is my teacher."

- George Whitman

Acknowledgments

I read the book *Learned Optimism* by Dr. Martin Selig-man when I was in my early 20's, which set me on the path to becoming a Life Coach. I had the honor of studying Positive Psychology under Dr. Seligman, and consider him to be one of my greatest teachers. I will forever be grateful for his words of wisdom and guidance in my career.

I am grateful for the expertise and passion of the instructors at The University of Pennsylvania's Master of Applied Positive Psychology Program. I would like to acknowledge Diane Reibel and Aleeze Moss for their superb instruction in the area of Mindfulness-Based Stress Reduction. The MBSR techniques have been essential to me in private practice.

The privilege of working with my clients is one of the greatest gifts I have ever received. I love my job and have learned so much from our work together! Interactions with my clients are what inspired me to write this book. I would also like to acknowledge my many friends for being there for me and encouraging me to complete this book. Their support and belief in me have truly kept me going when I needed it most. Many thanks to my editors, Roz, Mysia, Justin, Pam, Greg, and Linda. This book has undergone a number of versions, and eventually morphed back into the simple, practical, user-friendly guide that I had initially set out to write. I couldn't have done it without you.

Thank you to Micaela my gifted illustrator and Susannah my amazingly talented graphic designer for helping me bring my vision to print.

Finally, thank you to my children, Alexandra and Scotty. You are the light of my life. You have made me be a better person. The most important job I have is being your mother. I have strived to learn how to be my best for you, and in the process, I have become the best version of myself. You have been my motivation from the first day I met each of you.

Thank You!